Original title:

Twilight Echoes of the Mystic

Author: Lan Donne

ISBN HARDBACK: 978-1-80565-124-6

ISBN PAPERBACK: 978-1-80565-327-1

Threads of Magic in the Dimness

In shadowed corners, whispers weave,
Of secrets held from those who grieve.
A flicker here, a shimmer there,
Threads of magic dance in the air.

Softly calls the twilight's spell,
Where hidden wonders long to dwell.
With every step, enchantments trace,
The quiet heart of this strange place.

Through tangled paths of ancient lore,
The echoes of a world explore.
Each vibrant thread, a tale untold,
In hushed tones, the brave unfold.

A silhouette of dreams takes flight,
As shadows blend with golden light.
In stillness, find the heart's deep wish,
For magic's song is ever swish.

So linger now in dark's embrace,
And let the wonders interlace.
For in the dim, with hope's sweet call,
Threads of magic bind us all.

Riddles in the Embrace of the Night

In shadows deep where whispers creep,
The moonlight dances, secrets to keep.
Each star a riddle, shimmering bright,
In the embrace of the mysterious night.

Footsteps echo on cobblestone,
Carrying tales of the unknown.
Night's gentle sigh, a beckoning call,
To wander through dreams where wonders enthrall.

Beneath the veil of twilight's grace,
Nocturnal spirits begin to trace.
A flickering lantern in the dark,
Ignites the imagination's spark.

So let us wander, hand in hand,
Through enchanted woods, a strange land.
Where riddles bloom like flowers bright,
In the depths of the endless night.

The Allure of Secluded Realms

Beyond the veil where shadows dwell,
Lies a realm cast under a spell.
Whispers linger, secrets unfold,
In the heart of stories waiting to be told.

Winding paths of ancient trees,
Echoing laughter on the breeze.
In every glade, a treasure awaits,
As magic dances through old iron gates.

The allure of realms hidden from view,
Where the sky wears a vibrant hue.
With every breath, adventure ignites,
In secluded corners, our hearts take flight.

Night creatures stir as day turns to dusk,
Revealing wonders in their soft husk.
With every step, we drift away,
Into the realms where dreams hold sway.

A Canvas of Eclipsed Dreams

Upon the canvas of the night sky,
Eclipsed dreams weave and flutter by.
Colors swirl in a cosmic dance,
Painting hope in a daring glance.

Fleeting visions, soft as a sigh,
A tapestry woven with every goodbye.
Stars twinkle like thoughts yet to form,
In the quiet air before the storm.

Beneath the cloak of twilight's grace,
We gather fragments of time and space.
Where aspirations are born anew,
In the embrace of the night's rich hue.

Shadows whisper in the chill of air,
Carrying dreams that dance and dare.
In every heartbeat, the echoes flow,
A canvas of wonders we come to know.

Secrets Borne by the Night Wind

On the breath of night, secrets glide,
Whispered tales, like stars, collide.
Through the rustling leaves, a story spins,
Of forgotten places where true magic begins.

The night wind carries echoes of hope,
Urging hearts that yearn to cope.
In every sigh, in every breeze,
Lies a promise that time will seize.

Crickets serenade the tranquil sky,
As shadows stretch and dreams reply.
In the stillness, truths unfold,
In silver threads, the night has sewn gold.

So let the secrets dance and fly,
Borne by winds in the midnight sky.
For in the quiet, we might just find,
The hidden paths of the heart and mind.

The Serpent's Embrace at Dusk

In twilight's grip, the shadows sway,
A serpent coils where children play.
With whispers soft, it wraps a throng,
In silver tones, the night feels long.

Beneath the trees, old secrets stir,
As nightingale sings, a silken purr.
The stars ignite in velvet skies,
A glint of mischief, truth in lies.

The moon ascends, a watchful gaze,
Through tangled leaves, the darkness plays.
What lurks within the serpent's fold,
A story waits, both fierce and bold.

With scales of light and shadows deep,
The dreams of dusk we dare to keep.
In quiet grace, the creatures dance,
As magic weaves its fleeting chance.

Hold fast your heart, as night unfolds,
Embrace the tales that twilight holds.
For in this hour, our fate is spun,
In serpent's grasp, the night's begun.

Veils of Mystery in the Gloaming

Behind the mist, the world retreats,
In whispers soft, the mystery greets.
Veils of fog, like secrets kept,
In gloaming's hush, the shadows crept.

The last of light, a fading sigh,
As stars awake, they twinkle high.
A flicker here, a shadow there,
Awakens dreams that drift on air.

With every breath, a story flows,
In gilded dusk, the knowledge grows.
Entranced by fate, we stroll the night,
Enveloped in a dim, soft light.

What lies beyond, what waits undone,
In velvet dusk, the tale's begun.
With daring hearts and quiet glee,
We chase the veils of mystery.

Embrace the night, let courage soar,
In gloaming's grasp, forevermore.
The secrets of the dark entwine,
In whispered words, your fate align.

The Last Glow of the Setting Sun

The sun dips low, a fiery crown,
As colors blend, the day unwound.
In crimson hues, the skyline bleeds,
A promise kept, the heart still needs.

The gentle breeze, it carries song,
As shadows stretch, both fierce and strong.
With fading light, our spirits rise,
A dance of hope beneath the skies.

The fragile dusk, a moment dear,
In every heartbeat, love draws near.
The horizon whispers tales of old,
Of magic lost and glories told.

With twilight's brush, a canvas bright,
We paint our dreams in shades of night.
The final glow, a beacon's call,
In every heart, it binds us all.

So cherish now, this fleeting time,
The setting sun, a sacred rhyme.
For in its glow, the world transforms,
In love's embrace, our soul conforms.

Riddles Spun by Evening's Breath

In twilight's stretch, the riddles hum,
As evening sighs, we come undone.
Each breath of night, a soft caress,
We seek the truth in darkness' dress.

The moonbeams dance on rippling streams,
In silver whispers, weave our dreams.
With every gust, a question sways,
Lost in the maze of shadowed ways.

What tales are spun in whispered air?
In riddle's charm, we find our dare.
Each echo holds a secret's lore,
To pierce the night, to crave for more.

As lanterns glow with gentle light,
The heartbeats join in soft delight.
In quiet turns, the world revolves,
Each riddle spoken, a heart absolves.

So let us roam where shadows weave,
In evening's breath, we dare believe.
For in this hush, we find our way,
With puzzles spun through night and day.

Secrets Among the Gathering Night

In shadows deep where whispers tread,
The moonlight dances; stories said.
A hush encompasses every soul,
As secrets linger, lost and whole.

The trees conspire, their branches sway,
With laughter muffled, swept away.
Each rustle speaks of dreams untold,
In the gathering night, so bold.

Stars peek shyly, glinting bright,
Casting shadows on the twilight.
They hold the wishes of every heart,
A fleeting world, set apart.

With every breath, the night unfolds,
Its beauty wrapped in tales of old.
A tapestry of hope and fear,
In secrets shared, we draw near.

So linger here, beneath this dome,
Where every path can lead you home.
And find within the quiet night,
Your own heart's secrets, pure and light.

Reflections in the Faint Glow

In twilight's grasp where shadows play,
The world grows dim, a soft array.
Faint glimmers cast on silver streams,
Where silence cradles whispered dreams.

Each ripple dances, secrets beam,
A mirror holds the night's sweet theme.
The starlight drips like honeyed rain,
Creating magic that'll remain.

Beneath the arch of twilight's grace,
A fleeting moment finds its place.
With every breath, the echoes ring,
In reflections, old memories sing.

So sit awhile and close your eyes,
Let go of fears and silent sighs.
Embrace the glow that flickers near,
In the faint light, find what's dear.

Within this hour, peace will bloom,
As night enfolds the world's sweet gloom.
Where dreams and reality entwine,
In soft reflections, hearts align.

The Last Luminescence

Beneath the stars' soft, fading light,
The day surrenders to the night.
A final glow, a whispered chance,
In dusk's embrace, the shadows dance.

The lanterns flicker, dreams take flight,
In every glow, a hint of night.
A whispered promise fades away,
As night unfolds its velvet sway.

Each heartbeat echoes in the dark,
A flicker sparks a tiny spark.
The last luminescence draws us near,
In quiet moments, all is clear.

So hold this light within your soul,
Let it guide you and feel whole.
For in the shadows, there lies grace,
A gentle touch, a warm embrace.

As sleep descends, and dreams ignite,
We'll carry forth this tender light.
The last embrace of day will cling,
As nightingale starts to sing.

Sighs of the Nightingale's Lament

In moonlit woods where shadows breathe,
The nightingale weaves tales beneath.
With every sigh, a sorrowed tune,
Echoes softly 'neath the moon.

Her song, a tapestry of woe,
In melodies that ebb and flow.
She captures hearts with gentle hands,
As her lament through the darkness stands.

Each note dissolves in tender air,
A haunting call that draws a stare.
In every flutter, tales take flight,
In sighs of love beneath the night.

So listen close, dear wandering heart,
For every note is a work of art.
Within the weeping woods so grand,
The nightingale offers a guiding hand.

Embrace her sigh, let it unfold,
The stories whispered, the dreams retold.
For in her song, we find our place,
In nightingale's lament, we trace.

Pathways of the Gentle Night

Beneath the stars, a whisper calls,
Soft breezes dance through ancient halls.
Moonlit shadows play their tune,
Guiding hearts beneath the moon.

With twilight's brush, the world ignites,
Painting dreams in silver light.
Gentle paths where secrets lie,
Inviting souls to wander nigh.

In every nook, a story breathes,
A tapestry spun with old, wise weaves.
The night unfolds its velvet cloak,
While hope and magic gently stoke.

Among the trees, old voices blend,
A symphony where sorrows mend.
Nature hums a lullaby,
To cradle dreams as stars draw nigh.

So take a step, let worries part,
And embrace the night with open heart.
For in its depths, the dreams take flight,
On pathways forged by gentle night.

Light's Farewell in the Mystic Realm

When daylight bows to twilight's grace,
A dance of shadows starts to race.
The mystic realm with secrets old,
Whispers tales of heart and bold.

As sunbeams fade, the spirits rise,
In shimmering veils beneath the skies.
With murmurs soft, they weave their spells,
In hidden corners where magic dwells.

With every sigh, the colors blend,
A canvas where the dreams ascend.
Night's embrace, a fleeting friend,
Where light and darkness softly mend.

The stars ignite like scattered tears,
Carrying wishes through the years.
In this realm, where time suspends,
Light's farewell, as beauty bends.

Dance, oh heart, with shadows close,
In this twilight, feel engrossed.
For every end must hold a spark,
In light's farewell, a magic arc.

Murmurs at the Edge of Dream

At the border where dreams begin,
Whispers weave with a silken grin.
Curled in night's warm, soft embrace,
Echoes linger, finding their place.

The stars align in gentle songs,
Carrying tales of righting wrongs.
With every breath, the silence breathes,
A symphony the heart believes.

Through misty paths of dusky hue,
The echoes paint a world anew.
With tender sighs that brush the skin,
Murmurs dance, pulling from within.

In the stillness, visions grow,
Where hope and dreamers often flow.
At the edge of slumber's seam,
Life unfurls in a spotted beam.

As shadows blend with softest light,
A world awaits, both veiled and bright.
So close your eyes, let destinies scheme,
And hear the murmurs at the edge of dream.

Fragments of the Celestial Veil

In twilight's grasp, where wonders dwell,
Fragments dance beneath the spell.
Each twinkle wild, a story spun,
From cosmic threads, the night begun.

Echoes of time in stardust flow,
Painting skyscapes, soft and slow.
With every glance, heartbeats collide,
In celestial dreams, our fears abide.

Threads of silver weave through air,
Tales of lovers lost to care.
In every glimmer, hope ignites,
Whispering truths in tranquil nights.

Veils thin where silence takes its flight,
A glimpse of realms beyond our sight.
With quivering hands, we touch the grace,
Of cosmic wonders, an endless chase.

So look above, where night unfolds,
A tapestry of dreams retold.
Embrace the magic, let it sail,
Through the fragments of the celestial veil.

Spirit of the Gathering Hour

In twilight's glow, the shadows dance,
With whispers sweet in evening's trance.
The stars awaken, one by one,
As night unveils the day's long done.

A breeze arrives, so soft and clear,
It carries tales of those held dear.
With every sigh, the heart feels light,
Embracing dreams that take to flight.

The moon aglow, a lantern bright,
Guides curious souls through peaceful night.
In silence shared, we find our rest,
The gentle pulse of time expressed.

As laughter lingers in the air,
We gather close, without a care.
In bonds of warmth, our spirits soar,
Together lost in tales of yore.

So breathe the air, let go of time,
In every heartbeat, feel the rhyme.
As dusk unfolds its magic power,
We find ourselves, in gathering hour.

The Lure of the Mystic Horizon

Beyond the waves, the heavens call,
With secrets hidden, standing tall.
A land of dreams, where shadows blend,
In twilight's grasp, the visions send.

The horizon glows with hues untold,
Elixirs bright, both warm and cold.
A siren's song, so sweetly played,
Invites the brave, the bold, the staid.

Through tangled woods and starlit skies,
The mystic path before us lies.
Each every step, a story spins,
Unraveling fate, the journey begins.

With whispered hopes in heart anew,
On wings unseen, the seekers flew.
In search of truths, we dare to roam,
The horizon beckons, calling home.

So chase the dawn, let spirits rise,
Embrace the lure that never dies.
For every end, a start is shown,
A mystic tale, forever known.

Nocturnal Whispers of Forgotten Lore

In moonlit glades where shadows creep,
The ancient lore begins to seep.
From crumbling stones, a voice takes flight,
A tale of old to warm the night.

With every sigh, the echoes strain,
Through tangled roots, beneath the rain.
In silence deep, secrets unfold,
In whispered breaths, the past retold.

The trees stand guard, their arms embrace,
As memories blend in softest grace.
A flicker here, a shimmer there,
The mysteries dance upon the air.

In velvet night, the stories weave,
A tapestry we dare believe.
Each thread a path, each knot a key,
Unlocking worlds for you and me.

So listen close, let shadows speak,
In whispered lore, the strong and weak.
For in the dark, with hearts once sore,
We find the light in forgotten lore.

The Pulse of Sultry Silhouettes

In sultry heat, the silhouettes sway,
Drenched in dreams of summer's play.
With laughter bright, the night ignites,
A rhythm soft, in fading lights.

Through tangled vines, the secrets weave,
Where hearts collide, and souls believe.
In whispered tones, devotion blooms,
As passion swells in shaded rooms.

The stars above, in twinkle tease,
A dance of shadows, with perfect ease.
Through every glance, the sparks take flight,
In silent vows, the world feels right.

Each heartbeat quickens in the dark,
Embracing warmth, igniting sparks.
With every breath, the night unfolds,
A tale of love forever holds.

So let us sway, lost in a trance,
To the pulse of sultry romance.
In shadows deep, we find our place,
Together spun, in time and space.

The Last Dance of Daylight

In the meadow where shadows play,
The sunlight begins to sway,
Colors blend and softly steep,
As dusk calls the world to sleep.

Whispers in the gentle breeze,
Rustling through the twilight trees,
A golden hue starts to fade,
Leaving dreams, both bright and frayed.

As stars prepare their nightly show,
The moon ascends in graceful glow,
Casting silver on the land,
Where time slips softly like fine sand.

The last dance in warm embrace,
Draws the night with tender grace,
A lullaby for hearts that yearn,
As daylight's embers gently burn.

In the hush, a promise stays,
That night will weave its wondrous ways,
As dreams are born in starlit skies,
And hope anew begins to rise.

Melodies from the Silent Grove

In a grove where shadows meet,
Nature hums a soft retreat,
Branches sway with secrets rare,
Enchanting echoes fill the air.

Moonlight spills on silver streams,
Bringing forth the whispered dreams,
Creatures stir in gentle night,
Underneath the stars so bright.

Melodies of quiet grace,
Drift along in hidden space,
Notes that dance on evening's breath,
A serenade that conquers death.

Every rustle, every sigh,
Holds the tales of time gone by,
While the forest, wise and old,
Keeps its stories yet untold.

Here in twilight's soft embrace,
Life and magic share their place,
Each moment, a fleeting rhyme,
In the grove, beyond all time.

Enigma of the Night's Caress

When night descends like velvet cloth,
The world is bathed in shadows' froth,
Mysteries unfold with grace,
In the silence, we find space.

A moonlit path of silver light,
Guides the souls through endless night,
With every step, the heart does race,
Embraced within the night's warm grace.

In whispered sighs and secret dreams,
The universe, or so it seems,
Plays its part in cosmic dance,
Inviting all to take a chance.

Stars twinkle like scattered gold,
Stories of the brave and bold,
Each one holds a spark, a flame,
In the night's enchanting game.

In this realm where shadows play,
And spirits linger, come what may,
The night reveals its heart's caress,
An enigma of soft tenderness.

The Final Flicker of Day

As sunlight bows to evening's close,
The final flicker gently flows,
A canvas painted deep and wide,
Where dreams and dusk now softly bide.

The horizon blushes, kiss of fire,
While night draws near, its sweet desire,
A tapestry of twilight spun,
In this moment, day is done.

Shadows stretch on cradle's edge,
Whispers hold a silent pledge,
To guard the light until it's born,
In dawn's embrace, the light reborn.

Each flicker tells of tales untold,
Of hearts entwined and loves grown bold,
A final glance at day's delight,
Before surrender to the night.

In the stillness, hopes reside,
As starlit dreams begin to glide,
With every note, a sweet refrain,
The final flicker speaks again.

The Unfolding of Gentle Shadows

In twilight's breath, the shadows weave,
A tapestry of dreams we believe.
Whispers float on the evening air,
With secrets and tales they quietly share.

The trees stand tall, their leaves alive,
Guardians of night, where mysteries thrive.
They dance with whispers both soft and low,
A symphony sung by the setting glow.

Stars peek through a veil of dusk,
Painting the sky with a delicate husk.
Each flicker tells a story old,
Of lost adventures, and hearts of gold.

Moonlight spills on the cobblestone,
As dreams unfurl in the warm unknown.
Here in the hush, the world feels light,
The unfolding of gentle shadows at night.

Embrace the calm as dusk takes flight,
With whispered wishes that spark the night.
In shadows' grasp, the heart will see,
The magic of what is meant to be.

Scents of the Awakened Moon

At dusk, the air grows thick and sweet,
With scents that dance on twilight's beat.
Petals sigh in the evening breeze,
A fragrant lull that seeks to please.

The moon ascends, a silver globe,
It bathes the world in a fragrant robe.
Jasmine and rose, a heady blend,
In every corner, their voices send.

With every breath, the magic swells,
Of stories hidden in fragrant spells.
Through shadowed paths, the night takes flight,
Awakening dreams in soft moonlight.

Scented echoes of love once told,
Drift through the night, timeless and bold.
Each wisp a whisper, a gentle call,
To hearts entwined, embracing all.

So linger here where the night unfolds,
With scents that hold what the heart beholds.
In this enchanted, fragrant room,
We dance beneath the awakened moon.

A Symphony in the Afterglow

In the afterglow when day departs,
A symphony plays upon our hearts.
Strings of twilight, soft and low,
Guide us gently where dreams will flow.

The world exhales, a peaceful sigh,
As stars awaken in the sky.
Night's orchestra swells with sweet refrain,
Composed of rhythms, both joy and pain.

Crickets chirp their evening song,
A melody that whispers strong.
With every note that fills the air,
We find the magic of love laid bare.

The moon, a conductor in gentle bliss,
Directs the night with a silver kiss.
Every heartbeat joins the tune,
In this symphony beneath the moon.

So let us dance in the soft afterglow,
To a melody only night could know.
Together we weave our dreams anew,
In a symphony sweet, just us two.

Flickering Memories of Evening's Call

The evening whispers in fading light,
Flickering memories take to flight.
In the dimming glow, and shadows grow,
Old tales awaken, and feelings flow.

The candle's flame dances with grace,
Reflecting love's timeless embrace.
Each flicker holds a story near,
Of laughter shared and whispered cheer.

Soft echoes tread in twilight's spell,
In the heart's quiet where secrets dwell.
We gather moments, both small and grand,
In the tapestry spun by time's hand.

As night draws near, we lean in close,
To fond recollections we cherish most.
In the tender hush, memories weave,
A blanket of warmth that we believe.

So raise a glass to the fading day,
And the flickering memories that gently sway.
In evening's call, we'll always find,
The magic of love that binds our minds.

The Quietude of Forgotten Whispers

In shadows thick, where memories fade,
Whispers linger, secrets unmade.
Forgotten paths upon moonlit trails,
Echoes of stories in soft, quiet gales.

A flicker of light from ages past,
Holds the promise, a spell that lasts.
In twilight's embrace, all fears dissolve,
And in silence, the heart can evolve.

Through trees that sway in gentle ballet,
The winds scribe tales of yesterday.
Each rustle a note, a tender refrain,
Of laughter and love, of joy and pain.

In the heart of night, a solace found,
Within the stillness, hope profound.
Forgotten dreams in shadows await,
A world reborn, its own twist of fate.

So linger here, where echoes reside,
And let the whispers be your guide.
For in the quietude, truth gleams bright,
Revealing all wonders hidden from sight.

The Allure of Ancient Stars

Across the sky, like diamonds they gleam,
Ancient stories in every beam.
Galaxies dance in celestial grace,
Whispers of time in infinite space.

Each twinkle a tale from ages gone,
Of heroes, of love, and battles won.
They call to the hearts of dreamers lost,
Guiding their ships through the starlit frost.

In the cold night air, magic does stir,
A quiet promise, a gentle purr.
Hope woven tight in the fabric of dark,
Lighting the skies with each radiant spark.

The universe breathes, a timeless song,
Drawing the wanderers where they belong.
From dusk till dawn, they silently glow,
Where secrets of cosmos are shared, yet slow.

So gaze above, let your spirit roam,
Each star a reminder, you're never alone.
Embrace the allure of the night so vast,
In the dance of the ancient, futures cast.

Chronicles of Dimming Brilliance

As daylight wanes, shadows conspire,
Whispers of dusk, a muted choir.
Once vibrant hues softening slow,
Chronicling tales where silence can grow.

In twilight's arms, the world sighs deep,
Memories dance, though they often weep.
The stars emerge, a reluctant brood,
As echoes of laughter fade into brood.

Once blazing spirits, now flickering shades,
Like stories forgotten, time remade.
Yet in the dim, a soft glow persists,
A tender reminder in shadows' twist.

Within the dusk, resilience shines bright,
Fading yet fierce, a bittersweet light.
Chronicles written in hearts that persist,
In the depth of the quiet, the dreams still exist.

So gather the whispers from darkness and pain,
For brilliance may dim, but never is slain.
In the chronicles penned by the hands of the night,
Lies a promise of dawn's ever-lasting light.

The Dance of Celestial Harmonies

In cosmic currents, the planets sway,
A celestial dance in night's ballet.
With stars as partners, they twirl and spin,
In harmony woven, a song within.

The moon hums softly its silver tune,
As galaxies twinkle, bright as noon.
Rhythms of stardust, of pulse and grace,
Whispers of wonder in the vast of space.

Constellations weave stories with light,
A tapestry rich in the depths of night.
Each flicker a step in the grand design,
Echoing symphonies, divine and fine.

From comets that soar to black holes' embrace,
The universe dances at a leisurely pace.
In this grand spectacle, hearts intertwine,
Finding solace in rhythm, by fate's design.

So let the music of stars fill your soul,
With every heartbeat, allow the whole.
For in the dance of the celestial formed,
Lies the spirit of magic, forever transformed.

Dancers in the Softening Shade

In twilight's embrace, they twirl and sway,
Whispers of magic in the fading day.
Moonlight spills soft on their silken gowns,
A ballet of shadows in dusk's quiet towns.

With laughter that sparkles like dew on leaves,
They glide through the night, as the world believes.
Each step they take tells a story unsung,
A tale of the night where the heart stays young.

The Enigma of Dusk's Caress

Beneath the arch of the sky so wide,
The sun dips low, where secrets abide.
Shadows stretch long, in hues of deep blue,
The mystery thickens, tonight feels so new.

A rustle of leaves sings a lullaby sweet,
As night wraps the world in its silken sheet.
Stars blink to life, like eyes full of dreams,
Guardians of secrets in silver moonbeams.

Harmonies of the Waning Day

In the glow of the dusk, colors softly merge,
Melodies linger, like whispers that surge.
Nature conducts, with a delicate hand,
Each note, a story from a distant land.

The river reflects the deepening skies,
A symphony played where the quiet lies.
Echoes of laughter entwine with the breeze,
In the chorus of evening, the heart finds ease.

Dreams in the Silvery Haze

As twilight descends, a soft silver mist,
Wraps the world tight in fairy tale bliss.
Memory dances on whispers of air,
A tapestry woven with dreams laid bare.

The moon spins stories that softly unfold,
Of wishes and hopes like treasures of gold.
In this enchanted moment, lost in a gaze,
We find ourselves drifting through silvery haze.

Messages from the Silent Vale

In the valley where whispers dwell,
Secrets sleep beneath the swell.
In twilight's grasp, shadows unfold,
Silent stories waiting to be told.

Moss-covered stones, a gentle sigh,
Carrying tales from days gone by.
Amidst the trees, a soft refrain,
Echoes linger, lost in the rain.

Moonbeams weave a silver thread,
Binding dreams in the night ahead.
Through rustling leaves, a call so clear,
Messages drift, for hearts to hear.

Each breeze stirs a memory spent,
Reminding us of time's intent.
In silence, truths begin to bloom,
Emerging gently from timeless gloom.

So wander deep where soft paths lie,
Where nature's secrets do not die.
In the vale, let your spirit stray,
For the silent calls, if you'll stay.

The Golden Hour's Soliloquy

As daylight bows with a gilded grace,
The sun ignites the evening's face.
Colors mingle, a painter's dream,
Whispers soft in the twilight's gleam.

Shadows dance on the cobblestone,
Each moment cherished, never alone.
Time stretches thin, like a warm embrace,
In the golden hour, we find our place.

Birds take flight, their songs ignite,
Melodies woven in fading light.
A fleeting glance, a secret shared,
In every heartbeat, love is declared.

The world holds still, as night draws near,
In this hour, we cast off fear.
Hope blossoms like flowers in bloom,
Beneath the stars, dispelling gloom.

So linger long, as shadows blend,
In the day's farewell, let joys extend.
For in this hour, our hearts take wing,
The golden whispers of everything.

Echoes of the Deepening Blue

Beneath the waves where silence reigns,
A world awaits, adorned with chains.
Colors dance in the ocean's sway,
Echoes hum of a time gone stray.

The moonlight spills on the azure sea,
Bringing forth whispers of mystery.
Shells lie scattered, tales untold,
Holding secrets of ages old.

As currents shift, a song will rise,
Stirring depths with ancient cries.
In the deepening blue, we find our place,
Among the waves, a grand embrace.

Stars reflect on the water's skin,
Remnants of dreams that dare begin.
In every ripple, life does flow,
In echoes of blue, our spirits grow.

So dive beneath the hidden sheen,
To realms where wonder reigns supreme.
For deep in blue, our souls take flight,
In the depths, we ignite the night.

Fantasies Wrapped in Mist

In the morning's soft embrace,
A world emerges, filled with grace.
Veils of mist weave through the trees,
Carrying whispers on the breeze.

Each footstep leaves a tale untold,
In fantasies where dreams unfold.
The fog wraps close like a lover's kiss,
In this quiet moment, there's sweet bliss.

A silver glimmer in the haze,
Hints of magic in where we gaze.
In gardens hidden from the sun,
Where mysteries linger, never done.

With every swirl, a story breathes,
In the mist, all hope believes.
So wade through clouds, so gently spun,
For here in dreams, we are all one.

So chase the light through twilight's seam,
In that misty dance of every dream.
For in each fog, hope intertwines,
With fantasies wrapped in ancient lines.

Solitude in the Ember Glow

In a corner, shadows play,
Whispers echo, fading day.
Candles flicker, tales unwind,
Dreams held close, yet undefined.

Within the warmth, a heart beats slow,
Craving solace, ebb and flow.
Stars peek through, a tender gaze,
Ember's light, in twilight's haze.

Time slips softly, like a sigh,
Moments pass, yet never die.
Memories woven, thread by thread,
In this sanctuary, quietly bred.

Lingering scents of fires aglow,
Each flicker, a story to bestow.
Silence speaks in hushed refrain,
Solitude's embrace, a gentle pain.

But here I find a peace so sweet,
In the ember glow, my heart's retreat.
A world outside, both grand and vast,
Yet in this moment, I am cast.

Guardians of the Night's Secret

In the depths where shadows creep,
Guardians gather, vigil keep.
Moonlit whispers swirl around,
In secrets lost, they are found.

Eyes like lanterns, bright and keen,
Watching over all unseen.
The breeze, a shiver, soft and low,
Speaking truths in the night's flow.

Stars are sentinels, glowing bright,
Holding tales of day and night.
With every flicker, stories told,
Of dreams and wishes, young and old.

In darkness, courage springs to life,
Guardians wield their calm in strife.
Loyal hearts in every breath,
Defending hope, defying death.

So when the shadows draw near,
Fear not, for they are ever here.
In night's embrace, we find our way,
Guardians guide us, come what may.

The Lament of Dusk's Daughters

In twilight's breath, the daughters weep,
For dreams once bright, now secrets keep.
Veils of purple, cloaked in sighs,
Softly fading as daylight dies.

With gentle hands, they weave their song,
Of times when nights felt pure and strong.
Through silken strands, their shadows glide,
Wishing for the dreams they bide.

Lamenting stars that lost their glow,
In scattered hopes, the memories flow.
For every wish that slipped away,
A bittersweet note in their ballet.

Yet in their woe, a strength emerges,
As night's bright tide humbly purges.
With every sorrow, deeper roots,
The dusk's daughters find their truths.

So as the heavens dim and fade,
Their voices rise, a serenade.
For in their grief, a promise lies,
Of dawn reborn beyond the skies.

When Dreams Drift in the Shade

When dreams drift softly in the shade,
A tapestry of hopes displayed.
Whispers echo, secrets sigh,
Underneath the starlit sky.

In twilight's hold, where shadows blend,
Magic stirs, a timeless trend.
Close your eyes, let visions soar,
In the stillness, seek for more.

Beneath the branches, freedom calls,
Each fleeting thought, a treasure sprawls.
In gentle breezes, laughter sings,
Awakening the heart's true wings.

So linger long in quiet dreams,
Where everything is not as it seems.
For in the shade, a world unfolds,
Of glimmering paths and stories bold.

When dreams drift softly, take your flight,
Embrace the magic of the night.
For in each heart, a dream remains,
A whispered hope that still sustains.

Enigma of the Chromatic Night

In shadows cast where colors bloom,
A whisper stirs the velvet gloom.
The moon, a gem in twilight's hand,
Spills secrets soft across the land.

Colors clash in a vibrant dance,
Mysteries woven in every glance.
Stars twinkle with a knowing light,
Painting dreams in the hues of night.

The air is thick with tales untold,
Of daring voyages and hearts bold.
Crimson, azure, emerald bright,
A tapestry of pure delight.

With every breath, the night unfolds,
A tale of magic that never grows old.
In silken threads of the darkened sky,
Wonder whispers as time drifts by.

Enigma wrapped in fragile grace,
In chromatic splendor, we find our place.
Embrace the night, let your spirit soar,
In the chromatic night, forever explore.

Reveries Beneath the Silent Stars

Beneath the stars, in quiet repose,
Dreams awaken, softly they doze.
A sigh escapes the cosmic sea,
In reverie, we yearn to be free.

Whispers travel on the cool night breeze,
Tales woven in the dances of trees.
The universe hums a lullaby sweet,
Where every heartbeat finds its beat.

Shooting stars trace paths of light,
In a canvas drawn by the moon's delight.
Echoes of laughter swirl in the dark,
While night creatures sing their tranquil lark.

Time slips softly, a fleeting grace,
Each moment a tender, timeless embrace.
Awash in dreams, we drift and glide,
In cosmic currents, our souls abide.

Reveries hold the essence of night,
Each flicker and pulse a guiding light.
Beneath the stars, our spirits roam,
Finding solace, in night, our home.

The Underbelly of the Deepening Blue

Beneath the waves, the secrets lie,
In whispers murmuring, not to pry.
Creatures dance in shadows deep,
Where the ocean's heart begins to weep.

The tide swells with stories old,
Of treasures lost and legends bold.
Coral kingdoms thrive in gloom,
Their beauty masked by nature's tomb.

Echoes of sirens call from far,
Luring dreamers with each star.
In the blue abyss, where silence reigns,
Mysteries grow, and time remains.

Fathoms deep, the turquoise swirls,
Where shadows dance like lost pearls.
Every surge tells of battles fought,
In the depths where hope and fear are caught.

Dive into whispers, unravel the thread,
In the deepening blue, where once you tread.
Embrace the enigma, let longing guide,
To the underbelly where secrets abide.

Ballet of Fading Gleams

In twilight's grasp, the world pirouettes,
As day relinquishes its golden debts.
A ballet weaves in light's embrace,
While shadows gather at nature's pace.

The sun bows low, its colors bleed,
To dusk's soft fingers, like a gentle creed.
Each brush of light, a fleeting glance,
In the fading gleams, we find our dance.

Stars begin their whispered waltz,
In cosmic rhythm, where time exalts.
Moonlight glimmers on dewy grass,
As evening drapes its velvet mass.

Fleeting moments swirl like dreams,
In the quiet of dusk, life redeems.
The evening hums its sweet refrain,
In the ballet of fading, hope remains.

Let shadows twirl in a graceful sweep,
In the dance of twilight, secrets keep.
Embody the twilight, let souls gleam,
In the ballet of fading, we weave our dream.

Silhouettes of Dreams Under Purple Skies

In twilight realms where shadows dance,
We weave our hopes, as if by chance.
With whispered tales of stars above,
We paint our dreams, wrapped in love.

Beneath a canvas of vibrant hues,
The heart's desire finds gentle clues.
As fleeting moments drift like mist,
In every breath, a whispered tryst.

The twilight beckons, softly calls,
To secret realms where magic sprawls.
In silhouette, our futures gleam,
Awash in hues of every dream.

With every pulse, the night unfurls,
A realm where thought and beauty swirls.
In purple skies, our spirits rise,
To chase the laughter, the endless sighs.

Through tangled paths of whispered lore,
We trace the lines of what came before.
In dreams we linger, hearts entwined,
Under the spell of night defined.

Veils of Dusk's Enchantment

Dusk descends with a velvet grace,
It cloaks the world in its embrace.
With every shadow, secrets grow,
As glowing embers start to show.

Through winding paths where dreams reside,
The heart unfolds, no place to hide.
With every echo, whispers hum,
In twilight's grasp, the magic's come.

The branches sway like gentle hands,
In quietude, the silence stands.
In dusky veils of mystery spun,
We find a place where hearts can run.

In every sigh, a promise made,
In the dusk's soft, inviting shade.
Where dreams entwine with sweet delight,
And linger long into the night.

With each heartbeat, a story starts,
In dusk's embrace, it weaves our hearts.
A dance of moments, fleeting yet true,
In veils of enchantment, me and you.

Whispers of the Fading Light

The day exhales a soft goodbye,
As stars awaken in the sky.
With every flicker, tales unfold,
In shadows deep, where dreams are bold.

The whispering winds begin to play,
They weave through branches, soft and gray.
In fading light, the secrets bloom,
Within the dusk, dispelling gloom.

A tapestry of fading hues,
Where every star sings ancient news.
With open hearts and souls aligned,
In whispered breezes, truth we find.

Where shadows blend and time stands still,
With every thought, a quiet thrill.
In twilight's arms, we seek the spark,
That lights the way through paths so dark.

With every whisper, magic grows,
In fading light, the wonder flows.
A final dance before we part,
In every beam, a beating heart.

Shadows Beneath the Starlit Veil

Beneath the stars' enchanting glow,
Where dreams and shadows blend and flow.
In starlit moments, secrets weave,
A tender place where hearts believe.

The night unfolds its velvet arms,
Inviting us to heed its charms.
In gentle whispers, we confide,
In shadows where our hopes reside.

The moonlight dances on the streams,
It wraps our thoughts in gentle dreams.
With every twinkle, souls align,
In starlit tales, our hearts combine.

In silence deep, we find our way,
Through winding paths where shadows play.
With every heartbeat, life ignites,
In whispers soft, beneath the nights.

Together we will chase the dawn,
But for tonight, we carry on.
In starlit skies, forever bound,
With shadows close, our dreams are found.

Serenade of the Dimming Stars

In twilight's grip, the whispers call,
Stars begin to slowly fall.
A melody of dusk and light,
Embracing dreams that take their flight.

Through velvet skies, their stories weave,
A tapestry of hopes that breathe.
Each twinkle sings a haunting tune,
As shadows dance beneath the moon.

The night unfolds its gentle sighs,
Awakening the heart's replies.
In secret corners, lanterns gleam,
Guiding souls through a silver dream.

Fading echoes hold the grace,
Of those who ventured in this space.
With every glance, a spark ignites,
Serenades of star-kissed nights.

So let us drift on whispers light,
In the embrace of soft twilight.
For in the dimming stars we find,
The stories shared by heart and mind.

Echoes in the Stillness of Night

In the stillness, shadows grow,
Echoes linger, soft and slow.
Whispers dance on chilly air,
Filling spaces with silent care.

Moonlight spills its silver glow,
Casting dreams in undertow.
Each breath holds a tale untold,
In the night, the heart is bold.

Crickets chirp their melodies,
Rustling leaves in secret trees.
A lullaby in nature's keep,
Embraces those who wake from sleep.

In quiet moments, shadows speak,
Inviting souls who dare to seek.
The stars synchronize their shine,
In the still, the worlds align.

With every sigh, the night conveys,
A tapestry of hidden ways.
In echoes, we find our flight,
In the stillness of the night.

Radiance of Fading Fantasies

Ghostly dreams take shape and sway,
In a dance that slips away.
Fading lights of yesteryears,
Whisper softly through our fears.

Each memory, a glimmer bright,
Draped in shadows of the night.
Once so vivid, now a sigh,
As fleeting as the midnight sky.

Wishes made on stardust trails,
Carry softly through the gales.
Echoes of what might have been,
Resonate in hearts unseen.

Yet in this glow, a spark remains,
Holding fast to what sustains.
With every heartbeat, we ignite,
The radiance of fading light.

For even as the past departs,
It forever lives within our hearts.
In dreams, we find our fantasies,
Awakening from histories.

Chasing Shadows of Forgotten Times

Through ancient woods where secrets lay,
Shadows whisper, drift away.
In ghostly realms of time long past,
Echoed murmurs, shadows cast.

Footsteps lead to realms unknown,
Where lost tales are softly sown.
In corridors of history,
We chase the ghosts of memory.

Every shadow tells a tale,
Of love and loss that we unveil.
In nostalgia, our hearts entwine,
Chasing shadows, a silent sign.

With each turn, the light may fade,
Yet in our hearts, the dreams are laid.
For time is but a fleeting stream,
Where shadows dance and memories gleam.

So hold the echoes close and dear,
In the faint light, they will appear.
Through the veils of forgotten chimes,
We embrace the shadows of lost times.

Chants of the Fading Light

Whispers of dusk in the fading glow,
Shadows stretch long, where soft breezes blow.
Stars start to twinkle, the sky wears dim,
Nature's sweet symphony, a soft, gentle hymn.

Moon's silver fingers, they beckon the night,
Crickets are singing with all of their might.
Lulled by the magic that drapes like a veil,
Dreamers await for the hush of the tale.

Leaves dance together in twilight's embrace,
With secrets of beings who drift through this space.
Fires are crackling, their warmth like a spell,
In the heart of the woods, enchantment will dwell.

As stars glow brighter, the world holds its breath,
For shadows may harbor both life and soft death.
In the heart of the night, where the whispers reside,
The spells of old linger, the spirits abide.

So cherish this moment, before it takes flight,
Chants echo softly in the depth of the night.
In visions of starlight, let dreams intertwine,
In whispers and wishes, the magic will shine.

The Enchanted Hour's Lament

The hour is fading, a sweet, soft goodbye,
Time loses meaning as moments slip by.
Lost in the echoes of laughter and tears,
The heart of the twilight oft cradles our fears.

A breeze carries secrets, once spoken in dreams,
Of promises broken, of longing that screams.
The light fades to shadows, and shadows confide,
In the hush of the twilight, where secrets abide.

The clock's gentle ticking now's muffled by night,
As stars weave their patterns, so soft and so bright.
In this enchanted hour, the past gently sighs,
With whispers of longings that never say dies.

Time flows like a river, a current unseen,
Carving through memories, where what might have been.
With echoes of hope that still dare to unfold,
In this liminal space, where stories are told.

So hold close the moments, let them weave your fate,
For the hour's enchantment is never too late.
Darkness may linger, but light starts to creep,
In the heart of the night, where dreams wake from sleep.

Dreams Adrift on Celestial Winds

Upon winds of wonder, where dreams start to float,
Celestial whispers, like a soft, silver note.
Guided by starlight, that twinkles and gleams,
We wander through realms that are woven from dreams.

With each gentle breeze, on this magical ride,
Imagination soars, with the moon as our guide.
In the glow of the heavens, we chase and we chase,
Through the tapestry woven, of time and of space.

In clouds made of stardust, we leap and we twirl,
As visions take flight in this luminous whirl.
With laughter like ripples on enchanted streams,
We drift through the night, lost in luminous dreams.

Each turn of the heavens a promise of gold,
With tales of the unknown waiting to be told.
In skies painted softly by twilight's embrace,
The heart dreams of journeys in this sacred space.

So let your spirit dance on celestial tides,
For the magic of dreams is where true hope abides.
As night wraps around us like a warm, tender cloak,
We harness the starlight with every soft stroke.

Reflections in the Twilight Stream

In the twilight stream, where the shadows unfold,
Reflections are whispers of stories untold.
The water's soft murmur sings low to the night,
Where dreams dip and linger, all bathed in soft light.

Flickering lanterns sway down by the shore,
Each flame a reminder of what came before.
Memories ripple through the stillness they find,
In echoes of laughter, woven through time.

The moon casts her gaze on the glimmering waves,
Where seekers of solace find spaces that save.
In the heart of the dusk, where the worlds intertwine,
Reflections reveal what the soul seeks to find.

As stars blink awake in the vast velvet dome,
The stream hums a tune that feels eerily home.
In the current of night, we all drift and sway,
In the arms of the twilight, we wander and play.

So drink from the stream, let its magic awaken,
For each gentle bend holds a promise unshaken.
In reflections, we gather, we cherish, we dream,
In the twilight's embrace, love flows like a stream.

Where the Nightingale Sings

In the hush of moonlit grace,
A nightingale finds her place,
Her melody, soft and sweet,
Wanders through the quiet street.

Beneath the boughs of ancient trees,
Whispers ride upon the breeze,
Each note a tender, woven thread,
Binding hearts with words unsaid.

Echoes dance in shadowed light,
Stars above, a tapestry bright,
In her song, dreams take flight,
Mending souls through the night.

The world stands still, its pulse suspended,
As if the cosmos, wholly blended,
Listens close, in reverent awe,
To the magic of her draw.

Nightingale, with heart ablaze,
Leads us through the twilight haze,
Her serenade a guiding star,
Reminding us just who we are.

Portraits of the Dimming Horizon

Along the edge where daylight fades,
Brushstrokes soft, the sky parades,
With hues of amber, rose, and gray,
As sun takes rest, and shadows sway.

In this canvas, dreams take shape,
Each moment held, no chance to escape,
Whispers of the past unfold,
In colors rich, and stories told.

The horizon stretches, wide and fair,
A promise held in twilight's glare,
Waves of time that ebb and flow,
Paint the night with secrets low.

As dusk embraces realms unknown,
Each portrait speaks, yet feels alone,
Fragments of a fleeting day,
Smeared by fate, swept away.

In the silence, we reside,
With echoes of the day inside,
The art of night, a tender sigh,
As portraits whisper goodbye.

A Tapestry of Starlit Reverie

Underneath a quilt of night,
Stars awaken, one by one,
Weaving dreams with silver thread,
In a tapestry of what's ahead.

Counting wishes on each glow,
Beneath the moon's soft, tender flow,
Moments linger, time stands still,
As hearts embrace the quiet thrill.

The velvet sky, a canvas grand,
Where dreams are whispered, hand in hand,
Each twinkle a promise, softly sewn,
In starlit stories, we are not alone.

Mysteries swirl in cosmic dance,
Inviting each of us to chance,
To glimpse the magic, fleeting bright,
In the heart of the endless night.

A lullaby from worlds afar,
Guides us through, a wishing star,
For in this reverie, we find
Our place within the stars aligned.

Lullabies from the Fading Sun

As daylight wanes, a lullaby,
Whispers from the radiant sky,
Golden rays in slow retreat,
Wrap the world in warmth so sweet.

Crickets chirp, a gentle song,
In twilight's arms, we all belong,
As nature hums her evening tune,
Cradling hopes beneath the moon.

The last light paints the mountains high,
While shadows stretch and softly sigh,
Veils of dusk in tender grace,
Bring solace to the hurried pace.

With every breath, the world convenes,
In quiet moments, shared dreams glean,
As stars awaken, night descends,
A soothing balm that never ends.

So let us lay our cares aside,
In lullabies, let love abide,
For in the twilight's tender glow,
The heart will know what dreams to sow.

Emblems of the Wistful Dusk

As daylight fades, the shadows creep,
A world where memories softly sleep.
Whispers gather in the cool night air,
Emblems of dreams woven with care.

Stars awaken, a twinkling sigh,
In the heart of evening, the magic lies.
A melody hums through the twilight glow,
Painting the sky with tales of woe.

Misty echoes of laughter and tears,
In this dimness, our longing appears.
Holding onto the fading light,
As the dusk deepens into night.

With every breath, the world stands still,
Time dances softly, bending at will.
Embraced by the cloak of the dusk's own grace,
In its embrace, we find our place.

So let the daylight bow and yield,
To the magic that night's tapestry wields.
For in this hour of wistful dreams,
Reality merges with what it seems.

The Lament of Glimmering Fireflies

Beneath the shadows, they twinkle and weave,
A dance of light that makes one believe.
In the hush of night, their voices rise,
Soft lamentations in the starry skies.

Whispers of secrets in the gentle breeze,
Flickers of hope amid the dark trees.
They flit and flutter with stories untold,
In the gardens of dusk, their magic unfolds.

But fleeting their glow, like dreams in flight,
They fade away, swallowed by night.
Yet still they linger in our hearts,
A testament of when light departs.

In shimmering realms where they make their home,
Dancing through echoes, forever they roam.
In moments of stillness, their memory gleams,
A reminder to cherish our vivid dreams.

So listen close when the night is near,
For the fireflies' song is a call we hear.
A wistful lament, a treasure so bright,
In the heart of the dark, they ignite the light.

Hints of Wonder in the Obsidian Hour

In the depths of night, where shadows play,
Hints of wonder begin to sway.
The moon, a lantern, guides our way,
Casting enchantments that softly stray.

Whispers of magic, secrets concealed,
In the silence, our hearts are revealed.
Glimmers of hope dance in their trance,
Inviting the lost to take a chance.

In the obsidian hour, dreams collide,
Imagination's river flows undenied.
Each heartbeat echoes with possibilities,
Painting our souls with sweet probabilities.

Distant stars shimmer with ancient tales,
While nightingale songs drift on the gales.
In these silent realms, our spirits soar,
As beauty unfolds, forevermore.

So embrace the night, let your thoughts unfurl,
In the darkened corners, wonders swirl.
For in every shadow, a truth may bloom,
Hints of wonder in the night's quiet room.

The Guardian of Celestial Dreams

In twilight's arms, where visions dwell,
The guardian watches, casting a spell.
With every sigh, the world takes flight,
A tapestry woven with silver light.

Softly she lands in a whispering breeze,
Guiding lost souls with elegant ease.
In the hush of night, her purpose unfolds,
Protecting the dreams that the heart holds.

Stars twinkle wildly, their secrets unfurled,
As the guardian weaves through this sleeping world.
A sentinel of wishes on glimmering streams,
She guards the realm of our deepest dreams.

With tender light and a gentle embrace,
She nurtures our hopes with her timeless grace.
Each fleeting moment, a heartbeat she keeps,
In the sanctuary where starlight sleeps.

So close your eyes, let the night embrace,
The guardian's presence brings warmth to space.
For in slumber's hold, dreams shall glide,
With the guardian of dreams ever by your side.

Mysteries in the Gloaming

The shadows stretch, they weave and twine,
In whispered words, the stars align.
Beneath the moon's enchanting glare,
Unravel secrets held in air.

A flicker here, a rustle there,
The night holds tales beyond compare.
With every breath, the magic swells,
In gloaming's grasp, the wonder dwells.

A fleeting glance, a silent sound,
In twilight's realm, where dreams are found.
The world transformed, both strange and grand,
In shadows' dance, we take a stand.

The gloaming whispers ancient lore,
Of hidden paths, forevermore.
Through misty veils, we seek, we roam,
In every corner, find our home.

So linger long, as day departs,
In gloaming's arms, we bind our hearts.
With every dusk, a chance to see,
The magic in what's meant to be.

Embrace of Evening's Breath

The day exhales, the sun slips low,
In twilight's arms, the breezes flow.
The evening sings a soft refrain,
Of stars that dance in twilight's lane.

A hush envelops, calm and deep,
As day surrenders, night will keep.
The moonlight waltzes through the trees,
In evening's breath, a gentle ease.

With every rustle, dreams take flight,
In cloaks of dusk, we find our light.
An echo lingers, sweet and clear,
The heart remembers why we're here.

So let us linger, hand in hand,
As shadows weave their mystic strand.
In every sigh and every sound,
In evening's breath, our peace is found.

For love unfurls in twilight's kiss,
A moment caught in warm abyss.
Embrace the night, let spirits soar,
In evening's arms, forevermore.

Songs of the Dimming Horizon

The sun dips low, a fiery blaze,
Painting skies in amber rays.
A melody of hues entwined,
In songs of dusk, we seek, we find.

Each note a whisper, soft and sweet,
A chorus calls, the heart's own beat.
As horizons dim, the world holds tight,
To fading warmth that beckons night.

With every breath, the colors blend,
In twilight's grasp, our spirits mend.
A symphony of silence grows,
In solitude, our true self shows.

So raise your voice to stars above,
In songs of love, in songs of love.
Let every dusk bring forth a tune,
In dimming light, we find our boon.

For life is but a fleeting hymn,
In every sunset, shadows swim.
Cherished moments, soft and clear,
In songs of the dusk, we hold dear.

Hues of the Wondrous Eves

In every eve, a palette spreads,
Of twilight dreams and starry threads.
The canvas blushes, deep and bold,
In hues of magic yet untold.

With every brush of cooling breeze,
The world awakens, spirits tease.
In whispered shades that softly gleam,
We dance inside a twilight dream.

The stars ignite, a jeweled sky,
In wondrous eves we laugh, we sigh.
With every color, heartbeats blend,
In artful moments that transcend.

As shadows gather, spirits play,
In evening's light, we drift away.
Each hue a tale, each shade a song,
In wondrous eves, where we belong.

So revel in the dusk's embrace,
With every hue, find solace, grace.
In twilight's glow, we paint and weave,
A tapestry of what we believe.

Whispers of Dusk's Embrace

In the stillness where shadows creep,
The stars begin their watchful sweep.
Beneath the boughs of ancient trees,
A voice stirs soft upon the breeze.

Moonlight dances on the glen,
Whispers weave through trees again.
Secrets linger in the night,
A fragile world, both strange and bright.

Crickets sing their nightly tune,
While fireflies glow like tiny moons.
Every heartbeat feels like fate,
As twilight weaves its magic late.

A path unfurls in silver light,
Leading souls from dusk to night.
With every step, the dreams appear,
The whispers grow more crisp and clear.

In dusk's embrace, the heart takes flight,
Finding solace in the night.
For magic hides in every place,
If one would only seek its grace.

Shadows in the Lavender Sky

Beneath the heights where lavender glows,
The day gives way to evening's throes.
Shadows dance in muted hues,
As the sun shares its final views.

Whirls of color paint the air,
Hints of wonder, soft and rare.
Not a sound, save whispers low,
As twilight's kiss begins to flow.

Petals flutter, dreams take flight,
In the silence of the night.
Stars awaken, bold and spry,
Flecking softly the lavender sky.

Each moment holds a spark divine,
A fleeting chance, a secret sign.
Where shadows twine with shades of blue,
In the dusk, the magic grew.

So linger here, in this embrace,
Let the shadows find their place.
In the lavender's sweet goodbye,
Adventure waits beneath the sky.

Murmurs Beneath the Veil

In the hush where secrets blend,
Mysteries upon the wind suspend.
Veils of green and whispers pale,
Carry tales both fierce and frail.

Moonlit glimmer on the stream,
Casting dreams in a silver beam.
Beneath the boughs, the stories flow,
In every breath, the shadows grow.

Each step a stitch in twilight's seam,
Where thou art lost, a phantom dream.
Haunting echoes call your name,
Beneath the veil, not all is tame.

A flicker here, a rustle there,
In the stillness, the secrets share.
With every flutter, hearts will sigh,
And dance along, as spirits fly.

So wander forth with gentle eyes,
Among the murmurs and the sighs.
For in the veil, the magic waits,
To weave the dreams that fate creates.

Secrets of the Gloaming Garden

In the gloaming where shadows blend,
Garden whispers gently send.
Petals folded, dreams unfold,
In the dusk, their tales are told.

Crimson blooms and silver light,
Bring forth visions, bold and bright.
Every corner has a song,
In this sanctuary, we belong.

Rustling leaves sing lullabies,
Beneath the watchful evening skies.
Each secret held within each flower,
A testament of twilight's power.

In the stillness, hearts will find,
The gentle pull of fate intertwined.
As stars awaken, soft and clear,
The secrets melt our deepest fear.

So come and wander, linger near,
In the garden, magic's clear.
For in the gloaming, love will thrive,
In whispered dreams, our spirits live.

Glimmers of the Celestial Tide

In twilight's breath, the stars ignite,
A whisper soft, the world's alight.
The waves, they dance with gleaming grace,
As night unveils its velvet space.

A silver glow upon the sea,
Each ripple sings in harmony.
The moon, a guide, with gentle hand,
Steers dreams alive to distant lands.

The angels weave their tales of lore,
Of magic found on distant shores.
A tapestry of night unfolds,
As secrets of the cosmos told.

With every pulse, the heart beats true,
As stardust weaves, our spirits renew.
The tide shall call, with every sway,
In glimmers bright, we find our way.

So let us sail beyond the eyes,
Where hope resides in endless skies.
For in each spark and shimmer found,
A promise waits, forever bound.

Beneath an Indigo Sky

Beneath a sky of deepest hue,
The world transforms, a dream come true.
Where shadows mingle, softly blend,
And whispers float, as time may bend.

The clouds, like cotton, drift and sway,
In endless paths, they find their way.
As twilight hums its gentle tune,
We gather hope; we'll soar like noon.

With every star that lights the night,
Each one a tale, a guiding light.
The velvet air, so rich and warm,
Awakens hearts to every charm.

In indigo, the magic stirs,
As nature sings in sweet murmurs.
A canvas vast, where wishes fly,
A moment's dream beneath the sky.

So let us dance in twilight's grace,
And find our peace in this vast space.
For as the night unfurls its art,
We hold the universe in heart.

The Allure of Day's Retreat

As daylight wanes, a hush descends,
The sun bows low, the evening blends.
Golden hues melt into night,
With every shade, comes new delight.

The air grows cool, the breezes sigh,
A gentle hum, a lullaby.
In shadows deep, the magic weaves,
Of cozy tales and soft deceives.

The colors fade, but dreams awake,
In twilight's glow, the heart shall ache.
For in the stillness, truths reveal,
The warmth of love that we can feel.

The stars ignite, a silken thread,
A dance of light where dreams are fed.
The allure of dusk, a sacred space,
Where time untangles, joy's embrace.

So take my hand, let paths unite,
In day's retreat, our souls take flight.
For in the fading, we shall see,
The beauty in this mystery.

Murmurs of the Awaiting Moon

In quiet night, the whispers bloom,
As shadows stretch, foretelling gloom.
The moon, a pearl in darkened seas,
Invites the heart to flow with ease.

The forest breathes, a gentle sigh,
Where secret paths in silence lie.
Each rustling leaf, a voice so near,
A symphony that draws us here.

The stars convene in twinkling dance,
In cosmic waltz, we find our chance.
With every glance, a promise made,
To weave our dreams, though night may fade.

The waiting moon, with silver glow,
Shall guide us through the night's tableau.
For murmurings of hope resound,
In every echo, love is found.

So linger here, beneath her light,
Where magic lingers, pure and bright.
In whispers soft, our wishes soar,
As night enfolds, forevermore.

The Journey to the Enchanted Night

Under the veil of twilight's glow,
Whispers of magic begin to flow.
Stars awaken, twinkling bright,
Leading us deep into the night.

With each step, wonders unfold,
In the heart where tales are told.
Moonlit paths beckon and sway,
Guiding the lost who dare stray.

Creatures dance in shadowed groves,
In their eyes, ancient wisdom roves.
They share their secrets, soft and sweet,
As the gentle breeze hums to meet.

Time drifts like leaves on a stream,
Fractured moments, a fleeting dream.
Beneath the branches, magic swells,
In the stories only the night tells.

Hand in hand, we traverse the glade,
With courage found, we're unafraid.
Towards the dawn, we'll carry the light,
The journey awaits, in the enchanted night.

Unraveled Secrets in the Dim Light

In corners where shadows lie low,
Ancient secrets begin to flow.
Each wall whispers of long-lost days,
A haunting echo of forgotten ways.

With careful steps, we tread the chill,
The air is thick, electric, still.
Candles flicker with trembling grace,
Illuminating each hidden space.

Dust motes dance in the softest glow,
Guardians of tales that yearn to grow.
Unlocking mysteries dimly bright,
In the clasp of the velvet night.

Voices swirl like unbound air,
Carrying songs of those who care.
Through whispers, the past unveils,
A tapestry woven with human tales.

As we delve into each layered truth,
The present bends, a fleeting sleuth.
Together we forge a path so right,
Unraveled secrets in the dim light.

The Breath of Evening's Tapestry

The sun dips low, a fiery sigh,
Painting the canvas of the sky.
Threads of crimson, gold, and blue,
Weave together, a magical view.

As dusk enfolds the sleeping trees,
A symphony plays upon the breeze.
With every note, the world unwinds,
In the beauty that evening finds.

Stars unfurl like blossoms at night,
Casting their glow, soft and bright.
Each flicker tells of dreams yet born,
In the tapestry where night is worn.

With the moon's rise, shadows elongate,
Embracing the hush, we contemplate.
In whispers of twilight, hearts align,
In the breath of evening, we intertwine.

Together we walk through seams of light,
Embracing the magic of the night.
For in this twilight, love's refrain,
The tapestry breathes, free from disdain.

Fantasies Woven in Night's Embrace

Dreams take flight as the twilight calls,
In the land where starlight falls.
Each shimmer holds a story within,
A place where the magic can begin.

Clouds drift softly, cloaked in mist,
Carrying wishes that once were kissed.
In each heart lies a whispered song,
A melody sweet where we belong.

The moon unveils a secret path,
Leading us through its gentle bath.
With every step upon the ground,
Fantasies woven, love is found.

Under the canopy of the vast expanse,
We share our secrets, in a trance.
With eyes fixed upon the celestial stage,
Together we write, page by page.

So let us wander, hand in hand,
In the twilight's glow, we'll make our stand.
For in the night's embrace, we see,
A world of wonders, wild and free.

The Alluring Constellations

Stars above us shimmer bright,
Whispers of the ancient night.
In their dance, lost dreams take flight,
Guiding hearts with silver light.

Nebulas in hues divine,
Map the sky, a cosmic sign.
Awakening the poet's mind,
In verses where the starlings twine.

Planets spin in rhythmic grace,
Chasing shadows, time and space.
In the vastness, we embrace,
Magic woven, dreams interlace.

Comets blaze with radiant trails,
Carrying our whispered tales.
Beneath their glow, a secret hails,
Of love that never truly fails.

As we gaze at skies so grand,
Holding wishes in our hand,
In this night, together stand,
United by the heavens' band.

Enchanted Realms of Evening's Grasp

Twilight spills across the land,
Painting shadows, soft and grand.
In the dusk, the dreams expand,
As night's embrace takes gentle hand.

Whispers float on velvet air,
Secrets hidden, hearts laid bare.
Beneath a sky, so rich and rare,
Magic lingers everywhere.

Moonlight filters through the trees,
Carried forth on midnight breeze.
Every sound, a whispered tease,
In enchanted realms, we seize.

Stars emerge like gems so bright,
Kindling wonder in the night.
In their glow, our souls take flight,
Guided by celestial light.

With each breath, the magic grows,
In every shadow, beauty flows.
Wrapped in night's embrace, we chose,
To dance where only dreamers go.

A Melody in the Quiet

In the stillness, whispers play,
Softly singing, fade away.
Each note carries night's ballet,
A melody that lingers, sway.

Crickets chirp, a symphony,
Nature's voice in harmony.
Moonlight dances on the sea,
Inviting hearts to dream and be.

Rustling leaves, a gentle hush,
In the quiet, spirits rush.
With the stars, our dreams flush,
In this peace, we feel the crush.

Time stands still, so softly spun,
In the night, our hearts outrun.
Every heartbeat, just begun,
In this space, we are all one.

Let the silence fill the air,
Every moment rich and rare.
In the quiet, find the prayer,
A melody beyond compare.

Dance of the Elusive Fireflies

In the garden, twilight blooms,
Fireflies weave their lighted rooms.
Painting paths where magic looms,
In the dusk, their dance consumes.

Flickering like tiny stars,
Guiding dreams from near to far.
Whispers of the night, no bars,
In their glow, we find our scars.

Children laugh beneath the trees,
Chasing glow, a gentle tease.
In the warmth of summer's breeze,
We become the dance with ease.

Nature's jewels, a fleeting sight,
Twinkling softly, pure delight.
In their glow, we chase the night,
Elusive glimmers, hearts ignite.

As the stars begin to fade,
And the night's serenade played,
In the weave of dreams, we wade,
In the dance, magic is laid.

www.ingramcontent.com/pod-product-compliance
Ingram Content Group UK Ltd.
Pitfield, Milton Keynes, MK11 3LW, UK
UKHW021421230125
4262UKWH00028B/397

9 781805 653271